GOOD MORNING

DeMarlo Delatte

and

Dennis Vanasse

Introduction

Hello, my name is Dennis Vanasse. I'm a college professor, writer and motivational speaker. As a writer, I've traveled all over the United States speaking to people with incredible life stories. Although every story is unique, they all share three common bonds. The exploration of time, the experience of loss and the pursuit of happiness. For instance, I believe time holds us accountable for our decisions and actions, loss provides us with an opportunity to appreciate life and our pursuit of happiness gives us hope. In my first inspirational series "Good morning," I'll introduce you to a young man by the name of DeMarlo Delatte. DeMarlo is an American entrepreneur who started a successful business at the age of 30. After a chance meeting, I was intrigued by his positive outlook on life, his ambition and where it stemmed from. We discussed his past experiences and how they molded him into the person he is today. Subsequently, he was encouraged to share his story in the hope that it will inspire you to do the same.

Dennis Vanasse

Thank you

This book has been an incredible experience. It took an immense amount of work and would not exist without the invaluable contributions and support of the following people: Shayna Wilson is not only an amazing publicist and manager, but she is an exceptional friend. Her work ethic is unmatched, and I truly appreciate her support throughout this project. Thank you for your clear vision and direction as you represented me the entire process. Demarlo Delatte, thank you for sharing your story with the world. I appreciate your honesty with this project. Through your story, you are about to change many lives. Kerri Vanasse is not only my wife, but my number one support system. Writing a book requires a lot of time and effort. You are always by my side pushing me to excel. Thank you for believing in me. To my beautiful children, Sarah, Katie, Matthew, and Tommy, thank you for being my inspiration. It has been an amazing journey watching you grow. I am honored that you are always with me navigating through the process of writing a book. Keep reaching for the stars.

DeMarlo DeLatte

Thank you

I would like to thank the following people for helping me grow into the man that I am today. I am forever grateful to my mother. I was able to count on her as she guided me through my darkest hours. Thanks to my great grandmother Jean Woods, who introduced me to religion, and helped me develop my relationship with God. A special thanks to my grandparents, Lee and Lawrence, for teaching me so many valuable lessons. To my step-father, Antwon Grant, I appreciate the strong work-ethic you instilled and how you filled the void left by my biological father, Walter Greer. Thanks to my Aunt Dotty, for providing me with structure and discipline when it was most needed. To my cousins Jack, Malikka, and Monique, thank you for your unconditional love and guidance. I would like to thank my little brothers Daylen and Dallas for helping me become more responsible. I appreciate the never-ending support from my cousins Tim, Tai Hanson, Shay Shay, Robert, Danielle, Jermaine, Desmond, and Marcellus. To Darshaun, Chris, and Mike, I truly cherish our friendships and your ongoing support. Thank you to my sponsor, Joe Beirne, for walking me through the steps to recovery. A special thank you to Tony Valore for your spiritual guidance. I thank my children who truly love me no matter what and give me a reason to live. Much love and thanks to Tiara, the mother of my four oldest children. Thank you for always being there and never passing judgment. I would like to thank the team that made this book a reality: Shayna Wilson (Manager) Dennis Vanasse (Co-Author), Walter Tabayoyong (Graphic Designer), and Deborah Perdue (Book Designer). Most importantly, thank you to my wife Marika, who inspired me to share our story. I will love you forever and I cherish all of our memories together.

Preface

Good morning, a simple phrase we often use, so often we do not value the meaning of it. My name is Demarlo Delatte. I was born and raised in the "V" better known as the valley in Akron, Ohio. Growing up, winning didn't seem like an option for me. My neighborhood was plagued by gangs, drug trafficking and a poor school system. In fact, there was very little hope for us trying to survive in the small abandoned rust belt that once was, yet we found a way. I was your typical teenager. I attended school, played sports and admired beautiful girls. I had big dreams and I did everything in my power to pursue them at all costs. Unfortunately, I didn't always make the correct choices. I quickly learned that my environment was half the battle and who I chose to surround myself with was the fight.

In the year 2000 drug culture was on the rise. The use of heroin, crack cocaine, and prescription pills skyrocketed and swept the entire nation. Crystal meth gained popularity in the Midwest because it was cheap and could be manufactured at home. Physician prescribed opioids were easily accessible to adults and teens as dealers infiltrated schools and local social circles. The barrage of opportunities to partake in drug use was everywhere. As a likable, impressionable teenager, my encounters with drugs and alcohol increased my curiosity and propensity to indulge in an unhealthy lifestyle. The days of meeting up with my friends at local malt shops and arcades were over. House parties in trap houses and motels were the norm and there was no stopping it. While I saw my mother battle drug and alcohol addiction, I did not realize that children of addicts are eight times more likely to develop an addiction as well. In my youth, I was oblivious to the long-term effects of my substance abuse. As an adult, I would suffer the consequences.

GOOD MORNING

It was an autumn afternoon and my wife, and I were lying on the bedroom floor. I was tired from the immense amount of partying we engaged in the previous night. A few minutes later I got up to feed our children and as I walked past the mirror, I stopped dead in my tracks. I saw emptiness in my eyes and the reflection of my father. He once told me "Nothing comes to a sleeper except a dream, and sleep is the cousin of death." At this point in my life, not only was I unafraid of death, I welcomed it. My wife and I met in our early twenties at a concert. It was love at first sight. Eccentric, fiery, lively and ambitious are just a few words that describe her jovial personality. I still remember the first time we danced and the first time we kissed. She was beautiful, she was special, and she was mine. We had dreams of starting a family and goals of building a business. We were driven to be successful but as the adage says we worked hard and partied harder.

While most married couples celebrate their achievements with a romantic dinner or a movie date, we went to nightclubs and indulged in an excess amount of drugs and alcohol. What started as an occasional fun, turned into a lifestyle that drained me spiritually, emotionally and physically. As we continued to party, our binging was at an all-time high and our substance abuse affected our relationship in many ways. For instance, one evening following a routine traffic stop, I was arrested for possession of drugs. As a result, I was assigned a probation officer. It was a warning sign, but I was too oblivious to acknowledge it. After months of dodging my probation officer, I told him that I needed serious help, or I was sure to die. Without hesitation, he recommended that I call a rehabilitation center, so I did. Unfortunately, most rehab centers have a waiting list, so seeking immediate help isn't as easy as it sounds. For example, rehab centers are not free. For those that have access to medical insurance or money, the options aren't as limited. For those without medical insurance or money, it's life or death.

My wife was extremely sad that I agreed to enter rehab. She had negative connotations based on her mother's experience; however, she respected my decision to go. While I prepared for treatment, I began to inform family members and friends. Most family members were proud of my decision, but my closest cousin could not understand the severity of my disease. In my environment, many viewed addicts as either an unkempt stranger on the street or the homeless man sleeping under a bridge. That was not the case with me. My cousin had no idea how bad things were because I was deceptive about my addiction. To be honest, I deceived myself. I thought I could stop and start when I wanted to. While you're getting high, you don't think about your problems and when you are high, you can't provide a solution to solve them. As you come down from your high, you see the destruction around you and that increases your need to use again. It's a deadly cycle that I can assure you no one willingly wants to partake in.

A few weeks later, I was notified by the treatment facility that an available placement was open for me. My mother, who at the time was sober, supported my commitment. I'd seen her fight for her sobriety and I was inspired by her willpower to seek help. Like so many, I had questions about the process. By nature, I'm a stubborn person but I was vulnerable and the thought of losing my life made me humble. The night before I left for treatment my home was filled with mixed emotions; my wife would go from being sad to angry to extremely supportive. I felt so much pressure and guilt, maybe she was right, and I didn't need treatment after all. I started to think that I could do it on my own but that was my ego talking. The confident man she met was not the man that stood before her. With the holidays on the horizon, and bills multiplying, my wife indicated that I was running away from our problems. I assured her that was not the case and that everything would be okay. The next morning my mother arrived to take me to rehab. The following events would change my life forever.

The car ride to the rehab center was long as I sat in silence reminiscing about the circumstances that led me to this moment. I was anxious, fearful, and reluctant, not knowing what lied on the road ahead. To my surprise, the rehab facility wasn't what I expected. It looked like a horse ranch with a group of ranch-style buildings set off on the horizon. Upon entering the building, the staff greeted me with a warm welcome. They introduced me to everyone and gave me a tour of what would be my temporary home. As the new guy in the facility, other clients were quite accommodating. They shared personal stories, offered advice and checked in on me often. Their constant support was needed, it made me feel less alone and I was grateful for it. The treatment process was intense. I thought I'd have more time to acclimate to my surroundings after settling in, not at all. I woke up at 6 am every day and went on a morning meditation walk. I attended a two-hour relapse prevention class followed by an hour group therapy session. I was given three meals a day and a small amount of monitored recreational time. I did not have access to my cell phone or internet devices.

To be honest, it felt like prison and I was over-whelmed. I had no clue what I was doing or if I could do it. Adhering to responsibilities and keeping commitments was something I hadn't done in a long time. The process taught me discipline and accountability, key components needed for a healthy balance that was missing in my life. It was also an indication of how far gone I was and what I was fighting for, my sobriety. Not just for myself but for my family, particularly, my wife. I was deeply concerned for her. I needed reassurance that she was okay. We had never been apart longer than a week and I felt as though I abandoned her. It's one thing battling addiction alone, but it was another sharing an addiction with the person you love the most. When my wife and children came to visit, their presence meant the world to me. My wife was happy to see me, but she was stressed, and the pressure was mounting.

After all, it wasn't easy raising our children alone while combating her dependency on drugs. I conveyed to her that the process was working. She seemed hopeful and that was enough for me. Seven days into treatment, I began to see a change. My overall physical and mental health improved, and my mind was the clearest it had ever been. I had a lot of time on my hands to think about the past, my mistakes and the pain that I caused my friends and loved ones. I wondered if they would forgive me because at this moment I couldn't forgive myself. After decades of substance abuse, I finally came to the realization that I was an addict. I was fighting a disease. Coming to terms with my omission was embarrassing and painful but instead of taking the moment to reprimand myself, I reminded myself about the possibilities of a better future. I thought about the conversation my wife and I had during our most recent visit. We discussed relocating to a new city, providing a stable home for our children and starting a new life together. There were times when I wanted to give up and go back home, but she believed in me and she believed in us.

A couple of days passed, and I called my wife. A few minutes into our conversation I became irritated as I suspected she was under the influence. A brief argument ensued, and she hung up the phone. I decided to watch a movie to cool off but as time passed, I became agitated and worrisome. I called her back, and an older gentleman answered the phone. He informed me that my wife was rushed to the hospital. I immediately contacted my best friend and he drove me there. As we walked in, I flagged down a nurse and I asked for my wife's whereabouts. The nurse escorted us to a room where I waited to speak with a doctor.

The fifteen minutes while waiting for the doctor to arrive felt like an eternity. I couldn't sit still as I anxiously paced back and forth until he appeared. When he entered the room, he began to question me about my wife's prior whereabouts. I was dumbfounded. I conveyed to him that I was unaware, and I demanded to see her. And then I heard, "we tried everything, but your wife didn't make it."

The room went completely silent. The ground beneath me felt like a cloud as I became dizzy, on the brink of passing out. Without a second to spare, I hit the floor crying at the top of my lungs. My beautiful wife, the love of my life was gone. The next few moments were a blur. The doctor graciously escorted me to my wife's room. I noticed a white sheet pulled up to her chest, covering most of her body, her hair neatly combed back, with a tube down her throat from the attempts to resuscitate her. In disbelief, I began to shake her but as my hand sunk into her leg, I could tell rigor mortis began to set in as her muscles stiffened. I fell by her bedside, tightly grasping the hand of her lifeless body, as I uncontrollably wept, knowing that Marika was gone forever.

As I gathered my composure, I exited the emergency room and called the rehab facility. I informed the night supervisor about what transpired. He gave me the option of either staying with my children or returning to rehab. After a long pause, I took a deep breath and told him "I'm going to finish my rehabilitation." Life as I knew it would never be the same and at that moment I surrendered and asked the highest power to help me. When I returned to the rehabilitation center, I wanted to be alone. I was angry. I blamed myself for not being there and I blamed God. I didn't get a chance to say goodbye and that will haunt me for the rest of my life. I never imagined living in a world where my best friend was no longer with me. Marika touched the lives of everyone she knew, she was young, smart, funny and cared deeply for everyone. A light was taken from me that night and I didn't know what to do. I knew that if I returned to the streets, I would soon be joining her and my children would become parentless. The next few months were perilous, while in rehab I received news that my uncle passed away and shortly after my father did as well. I felt abandoned. I was fighting for my sanity and sobriety. In a short amount of time, I endured the most unimaginable pain and the only feeling I had left was hope.

In the pinnacle of my life, my desire for drugs and alcohol transitioned from recreational use to a necessity. I realized I didn't use drugs, they used me. While fighting my disease, I experienced the loss of loved ones, opportunities and time. It wasn't easy and every day was a challenge but I was determined. I vowed that the death of my loved ones would not be in vain and to never take life for granted. I started prioritizing my mental and physical health and focused on my children, goals and hobbies. I attended 90 meetings in 90 days and I began to treat the pain of my past as a moment in time as opposed to a lifetime.

Good morning, a simple phrase we often use, so often we do not value the meaning of it. My name is Demarlo Delatte, I am a 35 year old entrepreneur, recovering addict and I lost it all. However, through my failures, I relied on patience and hope and sought faith for perseverance. I suffered at times when I had the least and still offered my best. Most would call this a humble beginning, but I call this life. Every day is a new day, a fresh start to achieving your goals and becoming a better person than you were yesterday. No matter how bad the road was, don't let it deter you from the road ahead. So, wake up, and tell yourself "Good morning."

In loving memory of Marika Delatte

GOOD MORNING GUIDE

The following quotes, questions and activities are meant to inspire you and to help you fulfill a happier, positive, productive life. Change starts today. Live a life worth living and enjoy the journey.

—Dennis Vanasse

Self-Reflection

Self-reflection is vital to living a fulfilling life. Quite often, we don't give ourselves time to assess our thoughts. Asking yourself the right questions on a daily basis can awaken a voice inside of you that has yet to be heard. That voice, allows you to implement the necessary changes that are needed in your life. Honestly answering the following questions will help you discover who you are and what you truly want in life. As you self-reflect, you may also gain a new perspective and reconsider the way you live and view the world.

– Dennis Vanasse

The best journey in life is discovering your inner self. We all have many social identities in life that are only an aspect of us. You can be a parent, friend, sibling, colleague, or even a teammate. However, these identities don't truly represent who you are on the inside. When you begin to truly know your inner self, you will recognize your values, beliefs, and purpose in life.
– DeMarlo Delatte

Fear can be quite detrimental to faith when it casts shadows of doubt over our system of beliefs. The slightest bit of uncertainty can block your blessings. Life will be a continuous uphill battle when fear and faith are intertwined. It's important not to allow fear to take hold of your emotions. Fear can have a crippling effect that will rob you of your faith.
– DeMarlo Delatte

It may be difficult, but forget everything that went wrong the day before. Remind yourself that today is a new day and you have the choice to make it a good one. Although you don't have control over everything that may happen, you do have control over how you respond. Live your best life.
– DeMarlo Delatte

Have you performed an act of kindness for a stranger and if so what was it?

_____

_____

_____

Do you frequently volunteer to help others? If so, what do you do?

_____

_____

_____

What do you value most in a friendship?

_____

_____

_____

What values do you bring to your friendships?

_____

_____

_____

How would your friends describe you?

_____

_____

_____

How would your family describe you?

_____

_____

_____

What do you enjoy most about your friends
and loved ones?

_____

_____

_____

What is a great piece of advice you have taken?

_____

_____

_____

What's a great piece of advice that you've
offered someone else?

_____

_____

_____

What advice would you give to your
younger self?

_____

_____

_____

What do you want to change the most
in your life?

_____

_____

_____

How has your life improved in the past year?

_____

_____

_____

What would you like to improve
about yourself?

_____

_____

_____

What makes you smile?

_____

_____

_____

What makes you happy?

_____

_____

_____

Are you happy with who you are? If not, why?

_____

_____

_____

Name one thing you enjoyed about your day.

_____

_____

_____

What inspires you?

_____

_____

_____

What makes you unique?

_____

_____

_____

What is a defining moment in your life?

_____

_____

_____

How would you define yourself?

_____

_____

_____

Are you living your life to the fullest?

_____

_____

_____

Are you the person you want to be?

_____

_____

_____

What is your strongest personality trait?

_____

_____

_____

What do you appreciate about life?

_____

_____

_____

What are three things you cherish in life?

_____

_____

_____

What lessons have you learned in life?

_____

_____

_____

Did you learn something new today?

_____

_____

_____

What have your failures in life taught you?

_____

_____

_____

Do you have goals? If so what are you doing to achieve them?

_____

_____

_____

Have you helped someone achieve a goal? If so what was the outcome?

_____

_____

_____

Are you living a healthy physical and mental lifestyle? If not, what changes will you make?

_____

_____

_____

Name three healthy activities that help you clear your mind.

_____

_____

_____

When do you make time for yourself?

_____

_____

_____

How do you make time for yourself?

_____

_____

_____

What are you doing to contribute to
the environment?

_____

_____

_____

What will you contribute to the world?

_____

_____

_____

What made today better than yesterday?

_____

_____

_____

What was the highlight of your day?

_____

_____

_____

What does a perfect day look like to you?

_____

_____

_____

What is something beautiful you see every day?

_____

_____

_____

What is your definition of love?

_____

_____

_____

What does success mean to you?

_____

_____

_____

How do you overcome personal adversities?

_____

_____

_____

How do you alleviate stress?

_____

_____

_____

What are you afraid of?

_____

_____

_____

When was the last time you tried something
for the first time?

_____

_____

_____

Have you made a positive impact in someone's
life? If so, what was it?

_____

_____

_____

What would you tell your future self?

_____

_____

_____

How do you want to be remembered?

_____

_____

_____

Do you have any regrets? If so, what are they?

_____

_____

_____

What choices have you made in life that you are grateful for?

_____

_____

_____

How does your spirituality fulfill your life?

_____

_____

_____

How have social interactions improved your life?

_____

_____

_____

Self-Discovery

"Can you remember who you were before the world told you who you should be?" (Danielle Laporte) When you try new things, it piques your curiosity and opens up your mind to new experiences. This allows you to touch base with yourself about who you are and what you like to do. Give yourself time to see what this beautiful world has to offer. By discovering new things, you rediscover yourself. You will feel more energized, fulfilled, and proud of what you have learned about yourself and the people around you.

– Dennis Vanasse

Don't be surprised when an opportunity looks you right in the eye. At one point in your life, you will realize that you missed out on an opportunity. Maybe you weren't prepared, or maybe you didn't realize the opportunity was there, but you missed it. Don't stress out about the opportunity after it's gone as you will set yourself up for disappointment. Instead, be prepared to seize all future opportunities.
– DeMarlo Delatte

When you accomplish a task you thought was impossible, what more are you capable of? It's difficult to accomplish a task if you never try. When you challenge yourself to reach a new milestone, you have succeeded at something you set your mind to. As a result, you will develop confidence for reaching your goal and open your mind for new experiences.
– DeMarlo Delatte

When you are receptive to change, life will bring great experiences. It's important to have an open-mind when peers present new ideas. Too often we focus on the things that we can't change. However, when you begin to shift your mindset, amazing things begin to happen.
– DeMarlo Delatte

Tell yourself Good morning

◆

Participate in a charity walk

◆

Have a picnic

◆

Visit a local fair

◆

Adopt a pet

Set three goals for yourself

Try ice skating or roller skating

Sign up for a paintball game

Go for a walk in the park

Attend a sporting event

Attend a local art show

◆

Attend a free concert

◆

Practice meditation

◆

Complete a puzzle

◆

Go swimming

Go on a nature hike

◆

Take a train ride

◆

Wake up early

◆

Start a garden

◆

Host a bonfire

Volunteer at a local animal shelter

◆

Learn a new trade

◆

Watch the sunset

◆

Start a journal

◆

Ride a bike

Take a loved one to a movie

◆

Host a trivia game night

◆

Visit an aquarium or zoo

◆

Take a painting class

◆

Fly a kite

Explore horseback riding

Visit a history museum

Go for a scenic drive

Watch the sunrise

Take a bike ride

Study an ancient culture

◆

Study current events

◆

Take a road trip

◆

Go for a run

◆

Go fishing

Become a mentor at a local youth shelter

Start a blog on a topic that interests you

Give someone a compliment

Have a spa day or get a massage

Listen to the radio

Take a night to look at the stars

Visit a local historical landmark

Play miniature golf

Go rock climbing

Try a new workout

Attend a local theatrical play

Take yourself on a dinner date

◆

Take an overseas vacation

◆

Go to an amusement park

◆

Play basketball

Visit a local nursing home and engage

with the residents

Organize a neighborhood

environmental cleanup

Get involved in a community sport

Go to a bookstore and get lost

Volunteer at a local food bank

Set yourself up a photo shoot

Write a letter to yourself

◆

Learn a new language

◆

Create a family tree

◆

Watch a new TV show

Take an online educational course

♦

Buy yourself flowers

♦

Take a local pottery class

♦

Start a time capsule

♦

Plant a tree

Volunteer at a homeless shelter

◆

Take a martial arts class

◆

Visit your local metro park

◆

Take a yoga class

◆

Paint a picture

Learn how to play a musical instrument

◆

Take a dance class

◆

Create a photo album

◆

Give a gift to someone

◆

Go bowling

Help out an elderly or disabled friend, relative, or neighbor

Say something positive about yourself

◆

Create a relaxing new music playlist

◆

Start a club with your friends

◆

Get a new haircut

Donate old clothes to your local thrift store or

homeless shelter

Treat to yourself to an ice cream cone

Re-organize your living space

Make a new friend

Try a new recipe

Complete a project you've been putting off

Visit a veteran at a local V.A facility

Turn off your social media

Try a new food

Host a movie night

Participate in an adventure sport such

as skydiving

Strike up a conversation with someone new

Share your talent with a friend or relative

◆

Host a themed dinner party

◆

Purchase a new outfit

Self-Awareness

Beginning your day with a positive affirmation will put you in the right mindset. Journaling for 30 days allows you to process your emotions and increase self-awareness. This may change the way you view yourself, evoke mindfulness, and provide a platform for you to express your feelings without judgment or interruption. By consciously looking back over your journals, you will be able to track your patterns of behavior that impedes your personal growth and hinders your goals. Learn to be your own inspiration and your best inspiration.

– Dennis Vanasse

Celebrate the small accomplishments along the way. When you reward yourself for achieving short term goals, you will gain confidence and become more motivated as you strive for your next achievement. If you fail to celebrate an accomplishment, you are denying yourself the feeling that reinforces success.
– DeMarlo Delatte

When you accomplish a task you thought was impossible, what more are you capable of? It's difficult to accomplish a task if you never try. When you challenge yourself to reach a new milestone, you have succeeded at something you set your mind to. As a result, you will develop confidence for reaching your goal and open your mind for new experiences.
– DeMarlo Delatte

A positive attitude will bring new opportunities. When you have a positive attitude, you are more approachable and likeable than individuals who focus on the negative aspects of life. People will be more inclined to be around you if you bring a positive attitude to a conversation. This may open the door for future networking opportunities.

– DeMarlo Delatte

1

Every day is a victory.

_____

_____

_____

_____

_____

_____

_____

_____

_____

_____

_____

_____

_____

_____

2

Turn your limitations into possibilities.

_____

_____

_____

_____

_____

_____

_____

_____

_____

_____

_____

_____

_____

3

Seek clarity not judgment.

_____

_____

_____

_____

_____

_____

_____

_____

_____

_____

_____

_____

_____

_____

4

Change isn't easy just trust the process.

_____

_____

_____

_____

_____

_____

_____

_____

_____

_____

_____

_____

_____

5

Don't let a bad day become your worst day.

6

Don't let failure prevent you from success.

_____

_____

_____

_____

_____

_____

_____

_____

_____

_____

_____

_____

_____

7

Every obstacle brings you closer to triumph.

_____

_____

_____

_____

_____

_____

_____

_____

_____

_____

_____

_____

_____

8

If you haven't found happiness, don't worry, keep looking.

_____

_____

_____

_____

_____

_____

_____

_____

_____

_____

_____

9

Forgiveness begins with acknowledging the present and letting go of the past.

_____

_____

_____

_____

_____

_____

_____

_____

_____

_____

_____

_____

10

If you wait for the perfect moment, you'll wait forever.

11

Allow hope to fill your spirit.

_____

_____

_____

_____

_____

_____

_____

_____

_____

_____

_____

_____

12

Strive for the impossible.

_____

_____

_____

_____

_____

_____

_____

_____

_____

_____

_____

_____

_____

13

Allow yourself time to heal.

_____

_____

_____

_____

_____

_____

_____

_____

_____

_____

_____

_____

_____

14

You are enough.

_____

_____

_____

_____

_____

_____

_____

_____

_____

_____

_____

_____

_____

15

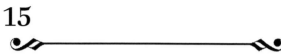

If you're moving in the wrong direction,
turn around.

16

A small effort is a great effort.

_____

_____

_____

_____

_____

_____

_____

_____

_____

_____

_____

_____

_____

17

Success is how you feel not what you have.

_____

_____

_____

_____

_____

_____

_____

_____

_____

_____

_____

_____

18

Your future is a virtue.

_____

_____

_____

_____

_____

_____

_____

_____

_____

_____

_____

_____

_____

_____

_____

19

Smile for those who can't.

_____

_____

_____

_____

_____

_____

_____

_____

_____

_____

_____

20

Your best is good enough.

_____

_____

_____

_____

_____

_____

_____

_____

_____

_____

_____

_____

_____

21

Find the positive in a negative moment.

22

Love yourself; you deserve it.

23

Begin to think about the possibility.

_____

_____

_____

_____

_____

_____

_____

_____

_____

_____

_____

_____

_____

24

Discover your inner confidence.

_____

_____

_____

_____

_____

_____

_____

_____

_____

_____

_____

_____

_____

25

Acknowledge your progression.

_____

_____

_____

_____

_____

_____

_____

_____

_____

_____

_____

_____

_____

26

Challenge yourself.

_____

_____

_____

_____

_____

_____

_____

_____

_____

_____

_____

_____

_____

27

Overcome negative thoughts.

_____

_____

_____

_____

_____

_____

_____

_____

_____

_____

_____

_____

28

Sustain a positive lifestyle.

_____

_____

_____

_____

_____

_____

_____

_____

_____

_____

_____

_____

_____

_____

29

Seek your inner peace.

_____

_____

_____

_____

_____

_____

_____

_____

_____

_____

_____

_____

_____

30

Embrace your new journey.

Made in the USA
Columbia, SC
22 March 2019